Life Cycles of Insects

Molly Aloian

 Crabtree Publishing Company

www.crabtreebooks.com

Author
Molly Aloian

Publishing plan research and development
Reagan Miller, Crabtree Publishing Company

Editorial director
Kathy Middleton

Editor
Crystal Sikkens

Proofreader
Kelley McNiven

Indexer
Wendy Scavuzzo

Design
Samara Parent

Photo research
Crystal Sikkens

Production coordinator and prepress technician
Samara Parent

Print coordinator
Margaret Amy Salter

Illustrations
Barbara Bedell: page 9

Photographs
iStockphoto: front cover (bottom right)
Thinkstock: front cover (top left); pages 8, 16
Wikimedia Commons: Waugsberg: front cover (bottom left)
All other images by Shutterstock

Library and Archives Canada Cataloguing in Publication

Aloian, Molly, author
    Life cycles of insects / Molly Aloian.

(Insects close-up)
Includes index.
Issued in print and electronic formats.
ISBN 978-0-7787-1278-7 (bound).--ISBN 978-0-7787-1282-4 (pbk.).--
ISBN 978-1-4271-9364-3 (pdf).--ISBN 978-1-4271-9360-5 (html)

    1. Insects--Development--Juvenile literature. 2. Insects--Life
cycles--Juvenile literature. I. Title.

QL495.5.A47 2013   j595.7   C2013-904039-0
                              C2013-904040-4

Library of Congress Cataloging-in-Publication Data

Aloian, Molly.
  Life cycles of insects / Molly Aloian.
      p. cm. -- (Insects close-up)
  Includes an index.
  ISBN 978-0-7787-1278-7 (reinforced library binding) -- ISBN 978-0-7787-
1282-4 (pbk.) -- ISBN 978-1-4271-9364-3 (electronic pdf) -- ISBN 978-1-4271-
9360-5 (electronic html)
  1. Insects--Life cycles--Juvenile literature. I. Title. II. Series: Aloian, Molly.
Insects close-up.

  QL467.2.A445 2013
  595.7156--dc23

                         2013023437

Crabtree Publishing Company

www.crabtreebooks.com   1-800-387-7650

Printed in the U.S.A./042018/JF20180309

Published in Canada
Crabtree Publishing
616 Welland Ave.
St. Catharines, Ontario
L2M 5V6

Published in the United States
Crabtree Publishing
PMB 59051
350 Fifth Avenue, 59th Floor
New York, New York 10118

Published in the United Kingdom
Crabtree Publishing
Maritime House
Basin Road North, Hove
BN41 1WR

Published in Australia
Crabtree Publishing
3 Charles Street
Coburg North
VIC 3058

Contents

What is an insect?

An insect is an animal with a hard covering over its body called an **exoskeleton**. The exoskeleton is like a suit of armor. It protects the insect's body.

exoskeleton

Insect bodies

The body of an adult insect is divided into three parts—a head, **thorax**, and **abdomen**. It has eyes, **mouthparts**, and **antennae** on its head. Its legs and wings are attached to its thorax. The abdomen contains the insect's **organs**.

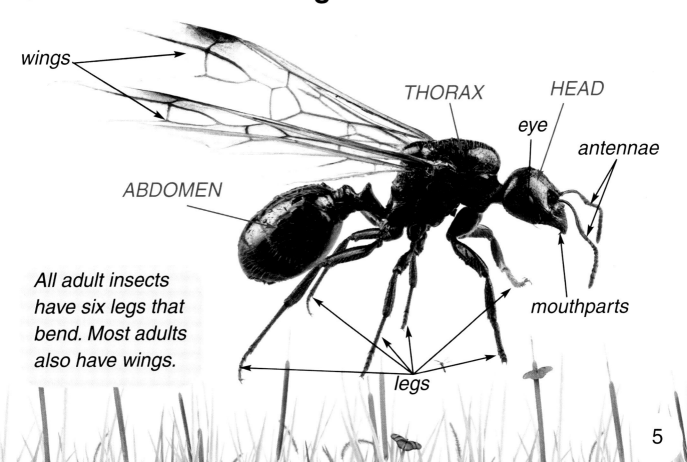

wings

THORAX

HEAD

eye

antennae

ABDOMEN

mouthparts

All adult insects have six legs that bend. Most adults also have wings.

legs

A life cycle

Every insect goes through a **life cycle**. A life cycle is the stages in an insect's life. A life cycle begins when an adult insect lays an egg. A baby insect hatches from the egg. The baby changes as it grows. Finally, the insect is an adult and can have babies of its own.

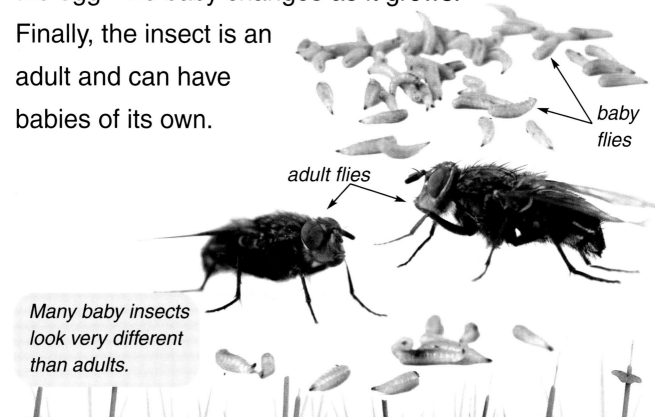

baby flies

adult flies

Many baby insects look very different than adults.

Changing form

Most insects go through **metamorphosis**. Metamorphosis is a set of stages, or changes, in an insect's life cycle. The word "metamorphosis" means "change of form." After the insect goes through metamorphosis, it is an adult.

This adult butterfly has just finished going through metamorphosis.

Two kinds

There are two kinds of metamorphosis—complete metamorphosis and incomplete metamorphosis. Almost all insects go through either complete or incomplete metamorphosis during their life cycles.

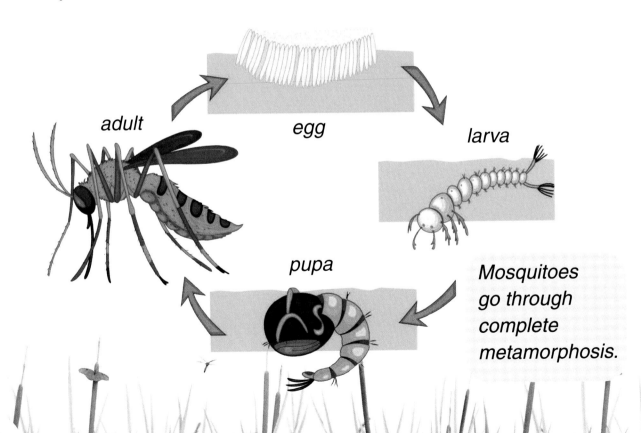

adult

egg

larva

pupa

Mosquitoes go through complete metamorphosis.

Changing in stages

There are four stages in complete metamorphosis—egg, **larva**, **pupa**, and adult. Incomplete metamorphosis only has three stages—egg, **nymph**, and adult. This life cycle is known as incomplete because there is no pupa stage.

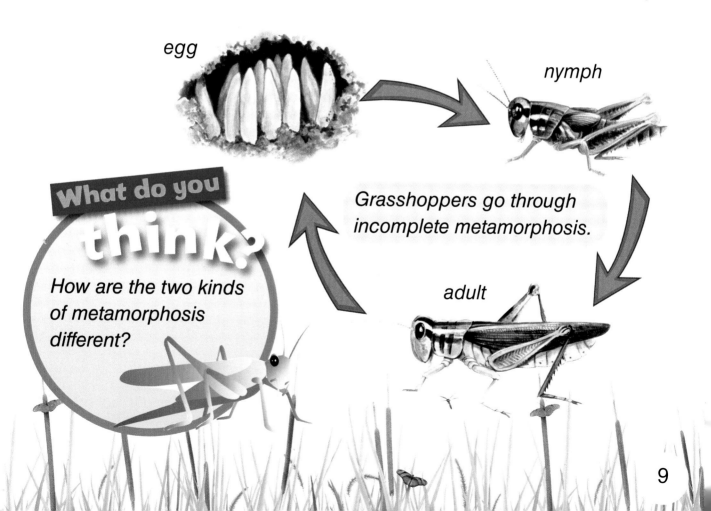

egg

nymph

Grasshoppers go through incomplete metamorphosis.

adult

What do you think?

How are the two kinds of metamorphosis different?

Insect eggs

Almost all insects start their life cycle inside eggs. Insect eggs are very small and often round or oval in shape. Many insect eggs are white or yellow, but others are brown or black.

This adult ladybug is laying eggs on a leaf.

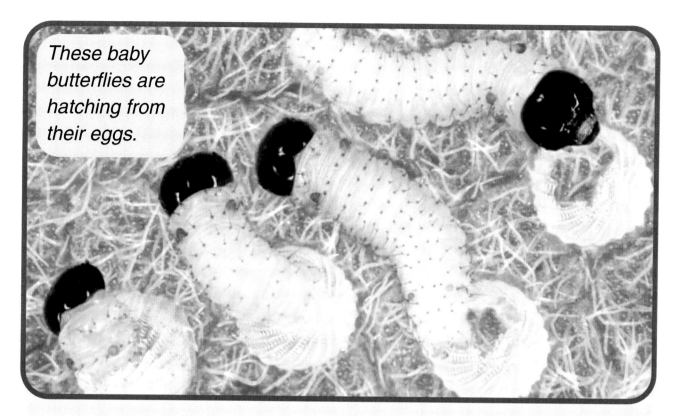

These baby butterflies are hatching from their eggs.

Time to hatch

Baby insects usually hatch in spring or summer when the weather is warm and there is a lot of food for the babies to eat. Many baby insects chew holes through their eggs. The holes are just big enough for the baby insects to crawl out of.

Learn about larvae

A baby insect that goes through complete metamorphosis is called a larva after it hatches from its egg. Many insects go through complete metamorphosis including butterflies, ladybugs, ants, and flies.

butterfly larva

adult butterfly

The larva of a butterfly or moth is also called a caterpillar.

Larvae life

These larvae do not look like adult insects. Many have no legs, wings, eyes, or antennae. Many larvae live on plants. Some live underground in soil. Others live inside wood or in water.

What do you think?

Look at the butterfly larva and ant larvae. How are they similar? How are they different?

adult

Ant larvae live in homes called nests underground.

larvae

New nymphs

An insect that goes through incomplete metamorphosis is called a nymph after it hatches from its egg. Dragonflies, damselflies, shield bugs, and grasshoppers are examples of insects that go through incomplete metamorphosis.

nymph

These shield bug nymphs have just hatched from their eggs.

egg

Little adults

When nymphs hatch from their eggs, most look like small adult insects. Many nymphs have eyes, legs, and antennae. Nymphs do not have wings to fly, however. Nymphs can live on plants, in water, or underground.

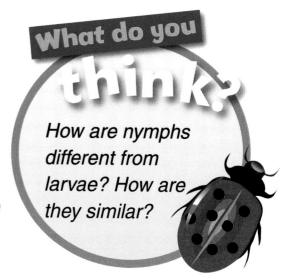

What do you think?

How are nymphs different from larvae? How are they similar?

Damselflies live underwater as nymphs and on land as adults.

nymph

adult

Eating and molting

Both larvae and nymphs eat a lot. They eat plant parts, such as roots, leaves, and stems. Some eat other tiny insects. Larvae and nymphs grow quickly, but their exoskeletons do not grow with their bodies. They must **molt**, or shed, their exoskeletons and grow bigger ones.

This beetle larva has molted its exoskeleton.

exoskeleton

Many molts

Most larvae and nymphs molt about four times. Some nymphs, however, can molt 20 or 30 times! A nymph slowly grows wings as it molts. After the nymph's last molt, its wings are fully grown.

What do you think?

What is an exoskeleton? Why do insects need it?

exoskeleton

This dragonfly has molted for the last time. Its wings have grown to their full size.

Pupae

When a larva is ready to become a pupa it looks for a safe place, such as under a leaf or underground. The larva then molts for the last time. Afterward, many larvae make cases or **cocoons** around themselves. They are now pupae.

This silkworm moth larva is creating a cocoon out of silk.

Changing into adults

The pupae change completely in these safe spots. They grow legs, eyes, and antennae. Some also grow wings. Many pupae do not move or eat during this stage of their life cycle.

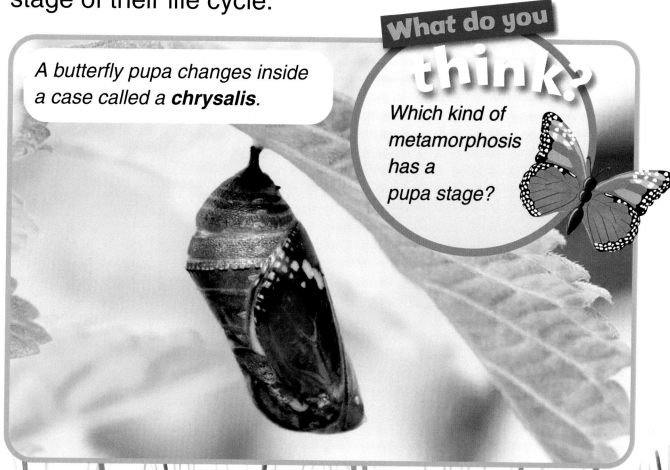

A butterfly pupa changes inside a case called a **chrysalis**.

What do you think?

Which kind of metamorphosis has a pupa stage?

Adult insects

When the pupae have finished changing, they come up from underground or break out of their cases. The insects are now adults. Nymphs become adults after their last molt. Adult insects have eyes, legs, and antennae. Most insects also now have wings to fly.

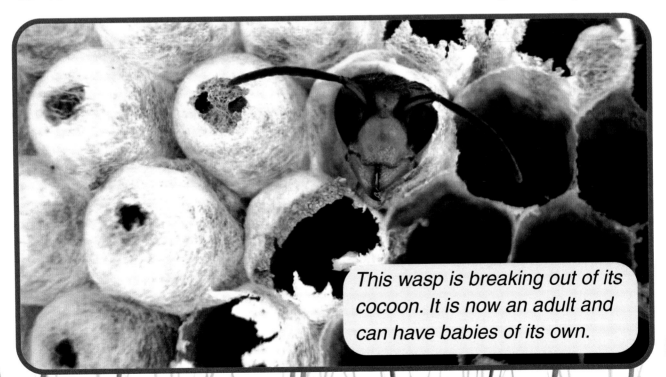

This wasp is breaking out of its cocoon. It is now an adult and can have babies of its own.

New food

Nymphs that live on land have the same mouthparts as adults, so both eat the same foods. Most larvae, however, eat different foods than adults. For example, butterfly larvae eat plant leaves. Adult butterflies drink a sweet liquid called **nectar** from flowers through a special mouthpart grown during metamorphosis.

adult butterfly

mouthpart

Compare and contrast

This activity will help you compare and contrast incomplete and complete metamorphosis. Review what you have read in this book. Then fill in this chart on a separate piece of paper.

QUESTION	EGG	LARVA	NYMPH	PUPA	ADULT
Which stages are in complete metamorphosis?					
Which stages are in incomplete metamorphosis?					
In which stages does an insect molt?					
In which stages would an insect be able to fly?					
In which stages does an insect eat?					

Learning more

Books

Linde, Barbara M. *The Life Cycle of a Honeybee* (Nature's Life Cycles). Gareth Stevens Publishing, 2011.

Kalman, Bobbie. *The ABCs of Insects* (ABCs of the Natural World). Crabtree Publishing Company, 2009.

Kalman, Bobbie. *Caterpillars to Butterflies* (It's fun to learn about baby animals). Crabtree Publishing Company, 2009.

Aloian, Molly and Bobbie Kalman *Insect Life Cycles* (The World of Insects). Crabtree Publishing, 2005.

Websites

The Life Cycle of an Insect

www.kidfish.bc.ca/cycle.htm

Insect Life Cycles—Amateur Entomologists' Society (AES)
www.amentsoc.org/insects/fact-files/life-cycles.html

Fun Insect Facts for Kids—Interesting information about Insects
www.sciencekids.co.nz/sciencefacts/animals/insect.html

Let's Talk About Insects
http://urbanext.illinois.edu/insects/01.html

Words to know

Note: Some boldfaced words are defined where they appear in the book.

abdomen (AB-doh-muhn) noun The rear section of an insect's body

antennae (an-TEN-ee) noun Feelers that help insects sense the world around them

chrysalis (KRIS-uh-lis) noun The hard-shelled pupa of a butterfly or moth

larva (LAHR-vah) noun A baby insect that hatches from an egg

mouthparts (MOUTH-pahrts) noun Body parts that insects use to gather or eat food

nymph (nimf) noun A baby insect that hatches from an egg and goes through incomplete metamorphosis

organs (AWR-guhns) noun Parts of an animal's body, such as the heart or lungs, which do important jobs

pupa (PYOO-puh) noun A young insect that is changing from a larva to an adult

thorax (THAWR-aks) noun The middle section of an insect's body

A noun is a person, place, or thing.
An adjective is a word that tells you what something is like.
A verb is an action word that tells you what someone or something does.

Index